AMERICAN SELFIE

American Selfie

by
Curtis Bauer

Barrow Street Press
New York City

Cover photo, "The U.S. - Mexico Border" by Ersela Kripa
Designed by Michelle Caraccia

Published 2019 by Barrow Street, Inc.
(501) (c) (3) corporation. All contributions are tax deductible.
Distributed by:
    Barrow Street Books
    P.O. Box 1558
    Kingston, RI 02881

Barrow Street Books are also distributed by Small Press Distribution,
SPD, 1341 Seventh Street, Berkeley, CA 94710-1409, spd@spdbooks.
org; (510) 524-1668, (800) 869-7553 (Toll-free within the US); amazon.
com; Ingram Periodicals Inc., 1240 Heil Quaker Blvd, PO Box 7000,
La Vergne, TN 37086-700 (615) 213-3574; and Armadillo & Co.,
7310 S. La Cienega Blvd, Inglewood, CA 90302, (310) 693-6061.

Special thanks to the University of Rhode Island English Department and
especially the PhD Program in English, 60 Upper College Road, Swan
114, Kingston, RI 02881, (401) 874-5931, which provide valuable
in-kind support, including graduate and undergraduate interns.

First Edition

Library of Congress Control Number: 2019934220

ISBN 978-0-9973184-8-7

for my family
of friends—you
know who you are

CONTENTS

I.

II.

III.

I.

"The greatest hazard of all, losing one's self, can occur very quietly in the world, as if it were nothing at all."
—Søren Kierkegaard

Euphoric

Maybe I should praise the mapped green
vast where the road I follow disappears

and the GPS triangle that is me begins
to twirl as if I'm not the only one confused

but then follows me into the expanse
in front of the car, in front of the declining sun

that in four hours more or less will glint the humping pump jacks
some oil shade of rusted, and I hope to be gone by then,

to have found some paved road I have never reached
down to touch but will to thank it and whisper *thank you*

like some hostage newly freed and returned to her country
kissed the tarmac in front of cameras before the neck

of her wife or cheek of her father or saluted
some officer obliged to welcome her home,

or I would better show my gratitude today by pulling
down the six coyote carcasses lining the property fence

I shouldn't have entered thinking it was a new way home,
past the gravel pit where kids from Ralls must come to drink

and fuck maybe their older cousins to escape their marriages
or to shoot cans or the sky and someone got so piss-drunk

he took off that pair of green denim jeans perfect
on the rack at Sears and less so each minute, out here

on a road without a name, a path really, and left them crumpled
on the crumpled dirt, the only green in this sea, this sea of red

earth a few still think what they do is farm
and therefore spend their money and hours

disking back and forth across the fields
like boats trawling the Salton Sea or

an astronaut on Mars who lost a special tool
in what wouldn't be called a field but something else

interstellar and spatial like *terra vasta* and this
is Texas so that might work

because the ground is vast and about
to blow around your face and

I haven't killed anything
with four legs and fur in years

though last night I misstepped again
and my friend the salamander

who clung to the wall near the kitchen
and watched me pass every day since July

jumped beneath a shoe and stayed
kissing the floor, as if euphoric,

having finally been released from the wall,
and I buried him in the trash heap I call compost

and I should drive back east to find those carcasses
now bristling in the evening wind and help them back

to that euphoric ground which adored them
and kissed each of their trotting feet.

Returning to a Moment

None of this surprises you now,
does it? I'm not sure I can know that,
I responded to myself.
Or I think I did.
I should have.

A friend told me to embrace
my disorientation here, to attend
to it and dwell in that state, make it
a daily practice, like walking,
or drinking coffee.

I've walked through this city
countless times these last five months.

Months ago, I couldn't
distinguish Bulnes from Pueyrredón,
prostitutes from neighbors on Córdoba.

I was learning to walk
through the nuances of this city.

Everything has changed:
I push into the *subte*; my wife
still can't buy tampons, women
think protest will change
something; hope, that lingering
scent jasmine blooms on a warm day,
but it dissipates
and I forget it ever existed.

I was surprised
when my friend told me she had cancer.

I thought then
I'd never not think of her.

Tonight Buenos Aires is a protest
in response to a recent murder:
a 14-year-old girl, pregnant, killed
by her 16-year-old boyfriend and buried
with his parents' help in their backyard.

Ni Una Menos, Not One Less.

I haven't thought of my friend
for the last month.
Maybe I've misplaced her,
the astonishment
that once joined me on my walks.

Can we always dwell inside
an unsettled state?

Early on I thought of her
as I explored. The night
I wrote her, her partner
responded, *My heart's heavy.*
I have to tell you Jackie died last Friday.

Death, I expected hers . . .
but I thought I'd see her again,
have an opportunity to tell her
about surprises here losing luster.

I don't know which way
to turn, how to understand
this. I had a stone

I was going to give her, but
I threw it into a pond and watched

the undulations calm,
erase the evidence
every ripple.

Selfie with Wind

I was invisible today and I spoke
long, eloquent sentences
no one heard. The oak leaves
shimmered and shrugged
off the heat. It could have been
dust speaking my name
or the deep breath of prickly pear
before it burst another bud
from its spikes, but the wind didn't
touch my back, tussle my hair.
It was an empty word and I am empty
like an oil drum rusting
in the fence line of a back field
brittle, dented, more empty
than an excuse given as
an afterthought or permission.
Tonight a dog kissed my wrist.
She was the first to address me
but the night was so deep
she must have thought *the air
holds an echo*, maybe thought
of someone who had passed
hours before scenting the alley
fence, or an announcement
of a man approaching inside the dark.

Evensong

God of Light, wake.
God of Lust, relent.

God of all things unknown
let me know just this once

how to love her, when, where,
and because I'm curious, why.

God of Pleasantries, Honesty, and Severity
I've had enough.

God of the Fulcrum, make mine strong
and remind me what it is You do.

God of Incarceration, my friend
is a good man, leave him be.

If you do
I will cut my hair.

God of Indecision,
forgive me for not knowing her better.

Finally, O Deity who art everywhere
thank You for these sins that keep me up,

thank You for
ham sandwiches and free porn, but

help me remember their names.
The one who promised

to let me make her honest.
She who showed pity

and led me down.
The one who let me

be unfaithful with another, the first foreigner,
the one who found me in a ditch.

She was kind, from Minnesota
and wrote wonderful letters even after I told her.

Is she a mother? If so, let her child
be good. Please.

The one in the ditch used me, but
I'd like to think I taught her something.

If You can, give me a sign:
was she from Denmark?

Did she believe anything I said?
It's too late, I suppose.

God of Forgotten Lovers, help me remember
if not their names, their faces at 3:00 a.m.,

remind me at unexpected times
of face curves and lines. Help me

remember when I walk home at night
with no one to hold. Help me wake

this sleeping soul, oh God of Light
when You wake.

Tonight I have one more plea.
There is one other.

Now her eyes are closed and
if I were there her hands would be

holding mine, if she were
here, I would not be asking for your help.

Lord, Friend, bestow your compassion
on this waywardness. Turn her away

if she comes to You. Tell her
You have met Your quota,

Tell her times are hard. Please
think of an excuse, say anything,

don't take her away.

Occupational

Even today—sun
rising, heating, setting—
grass in the cracked
asphalt grows. Some dead
are gone and some living
buy tickets for a matinee.
My kid cries out
the upstairs window. Her
mother watches a neighbor
fidget with her purse
on the street. I'm fine. The dog
is fine. Everything's fine.
The world spins forward
and no one controls it,
or the boy who sat on a bench
yesterday, his shoes stuck
to the gum on the ground,
his fingers sticky on the toy
in his hands. Someone thought
about control and made a call,
felt fear or the cause of fear
waited there in the boy's hands.
The word *end* means you
can leave if you've watched
a movie, or you close the book
and reshelve it, or you stop
crying. The drunk man on
22nd Avenue wants his voice
back. No one knows how
long he's been silent or how
to listen in when he asks
the chipped brick wall, *Is it*

the an-ti-ci-pa-a-tion or the act?
I want to know why I fill
with so much love
only sometimes. The plants
on the fire escape speckle
the alley with geometries
someone smarter could
turn into algebras of relations.
The sun is gone. The boy
is dead. His friend hasn't
started to stop missing him.

Obituary

This morning's news will note nothing
about your death, how a glass broke
from the ricochet in your chest. No soil

scent of what you will become will rub
off on my fingers. No report of nights
you slept on my floor, of the heat

those days we drank ourselves dumb,
of the billiard balls clacking and thumbing
soft along the bumpers. Of you nothing remains

but my selfish wishes, but me saying your name
forty-four times today. Yesterday I had forgotten
we were friends. And tomorrow—I know

who I am, who I've now become—and tomorrow,
of this I'm certain, or days after, I will forget again.

Selfie with Dust

There is a light I love, I loved
in the house where I was born.

Inside the door the foyer filled
with slanted light shimmering

cascades of particulates pooled
there, then burst, billowed,

and flowed through as if
having somewhere to go,

to fall a thousand miles more
or get out of town as I would

later, though I didn't know why
then bathing there in the churning

dust that tossed and stirred, stewed
by that light and heat into a form

like a body's embrace unfolding
upon me, holding me, emboldened

child inside the vigor of that space,
pulling out some courage to step

into that seething and dance
in the hands of dust. My hands

wove through it, cupped and
touched it. We embraced. I learned

what part of light I can become
floating, twirling, how

to step above the floor,
then out, then further out.

Cloud Study—a Grammar of Grackles

A half thousand punctuations
flap through this late October

morning. They quotation mark
the clouds, the clouds mimic them.

Negative space that does nothing
but deepen the space around them.

Like crows north of here, dawn
raises a curling wave of them,

a wave toward the sun's shore, or the far edge
of this town, at least. They wash over

trees, over sparrows and broken kites quaking
awake this morning on the power lines.

No children walking to school yet.
No laughter. But theirs, like metal

slipping on metal in the mechanic's
garage. Grackle, a color

darkened by desert light,
by cold. Rain turns black under them flying.

Mornings they don't punctuate the ground
but edit from above. Their eyes

dark moving within dark. A shine
there pulling in what is lighter.

They will outlast us who live here
growing their burrs and knots

fragmenting the sky. They are
always in front of a brighter day.

Each tree they leave floats in their wake,
joined to the earth by shared roots.

One Reason for Your Silence

No matter how hard I listen, I can't hear my wife's
voice. She lost it outside of town—west of there,

where trains stack up their great barreling chests
and smoke, and the wind whips grass and dust

scatters and fades into some older incarnation.
Once a Polish man told me about his rooms in exile

in a far corner of this country, their proximity
to the noisiest people in the world. Each night

when he sat to his solitary dinner and his books,
the noise of the earth would gather outside

the opposite wall he shared, guiltily. Even the fork
clink scraping across his plate left him. And his

breathing. Once he put his fingers in his ears
as if he were a child swimming inside a summer

pool alone with gaping fish and the song of his hands
through water, the dense thrum of pressure clinging

to him. Even the memory of his stretching chest
left him. He became heartless.

                              And that was enough
to learn how to stand outside the clamor and bustle

on the other side of a wall. I've never owned a sound.
I speak a name and the name is gone. Amnesia

might take this form—the soft tone of some man
seducing a woman is a murmur, a dog barking

to be let out or in only clamor, only noise gathering
and clinging to the walls on the other side. The world

keeps from some even the words on the page,
mute. When some rooms are demolished

their walls must finally give back a bit of beating
sound. Say one of those neighbors stopped

near there with his new wife, called up the child
he once was to show her how far his arm could throw

a rock, hit a sign or maybe the passing train. The train
may have blown its horn and the silence leached out

of the stone ping. The silence was then great between
the horn and his woman, and he needed to throw it away.

The stone hit the train, bounded back and she began
to speak. The train was quiet and stopped in the middle

of this vast flat, engines idling down to thin humming.
And from some shoulder stones in the road, bordered

by lanky grasses and loam that silence sifts up to a passing
car, through the seat, through the conversation suddenly

paused. No one will be satisfied with how this ends.
Because stories have an ending here; inside space

even a conversation can lose its way. A couple can fall
asleep angry, both certain the other stopped speaking first.

Neither consider the stone. And the stone sits untouched
in a cage of stars, a cage the night presses down

over the grass, and the voice of everything passing
by is swallowed up, until it isn't.

What Beauty Is, Is

The seam of your vein falling
up your arm raised to wave me

close, a stream blued this November
day when dawn light splashes yellow

on the pecan's rusted green pool,
en eddy of grass uncut after a month

of desert rain, this red earthed-
under juniper wash doesn't splash

over your feet any autumn, any breeze
drawing its hands through your hair

I don't know how to describe
                              because

if I call it straw I will think dry
and harvested fields in July, or brown

means the death left after frost's
long morning. Sorrel is a horse.

Chestnut a tree I would not know
how to pick from a buckeye,

which is darker, a shinier dark than yours
and I've almost forgotten I'm thinking

of you, of that cinnamon trickle
over your shoulders, too, to

your neck and the dust that must cling
to my lips when I kiss it. I can see

or taste nothing, but I know others know
I've kissed that tangle good morning, good

night, and some random good midweek
when you wave hi from across the street,

seeing me watching from the window
for you, the live oaks burdened with grackle

black between me and your arm
a seam in my day, that vein a seam inside

the seam sewing you tight to me when we touch,
which is what beauty is today.

In Praise of Maybe

A foghorn sounding through fog makes the fog seem to be everything.
—Anne Carson

It happened walking by, thinking about what's just beyond the maybe
hovering outside the reason I left, the maybe of this woman north
of here I could fall in love with if the sky were bluer than the ocean
every day or first snow fall in Buenos Aires at the end of every July,
that maybe, a fog I'd like to walk through

                           get lost in. This morning's
maybe the bodies on the sidewalk under the scaffolding, sprawled
in such a way I'm thinking half a block away what steps I'll dance to pass
between them and the dumpster, whether they will stop me, try to, or say
some simple words for coins or food or even help I won't understand and
therefore draw tighter the knot their attention makes around my neck,
                                          and

I don't fully see the man curled on a bare mattress, his bag his pillow,
only that he's a man who has made a home on the sidewalk. I forget him

25

or I'm to the point

as one must in this city, or I tell myself I must,

I don't think and instead see the bodies that worried me are children
entangled on mattresses and blankets in a game of cards, the oldest maybe
twelve, three boys and a girl, the youngest on his belly, crisp cards perfect
and gathered in his right hand, his left reaching for another, and he could
have pulled at a cigarette clinging to his lip while he mumbled and that
wouldn't have surprised me, and I looked back after half a block when
I heard a shout and clattering laughter and walked on,

and on my way

home from a shop where I buy coffee I was still thinking of them and still
just enough disoriented by living in this old city still new to me to walk
one block too far and have to circle back on a different street where I saw
a shoebox of cassette tapes cloudy on a window sill, and a deodorant stick
like the one I use and a blue Bic pen, and I saw them as out-of-place-like-me
objects and turned the corner and saw what I missed before,

the sleeping man

had turned on his stomach while I worried and wandered and now lay calmly, his head on his arms, a Q tattooed across one hand and a symbol on the other, a blanket covering him except his feet, which poking out from the blanket were sprouting feathers, white and soft and fluttering just so softly I remembered the breeze beside the traffic that maybe felt like something else in his dreams.

Loving This Woman—Three Movements

Sparrow chirps—
never enough, never
enough—and says goodbye
for us, tells me to forget
her held-back slap, thrust
that hand in your pocket
instead of around her waist
or into her hand. Sometimes
I don't know how not to hear
them. Ours isn't any kind
of permanent love. It knows
an end and how to walk out
the door and settle in
to a peculiar life somewhere
else for a while. It must.
Sparrows looking for food—
or is it tenderness—find it
on a companion's neck,
and they know what
to do with their feet.

~

Traffic hum in the dark,
like an overworked ice
box heaves in the next room.
Sometimes I can't tell
my foot from my arm. And
where, if any place, to place
my swollen hands. October, yard
yellow, like June, or any month
here. That loving this woman could

be like looking out a window
on the dead yard isn't romantic.
I hate the yard for how it looks
back at me every morning.

⁓

This is not where I want to live.
These words, not the body
I inhabit. *Nasty, unabashed,*
absolute, are words I want
hugging my waist. And I want
to inhale—*effluviant, ambrosia, sinister.*
I exhale *exhaustion, elegiac, Lisboa,*
amphibrach. If I were another man,
I'd stop before you, woman wearing
your hair just so…I like how that,
yes what you are wearing,
gives structure to your shoulders.

If I had a mother-in-law she'd say
Es la percha que hace la prenda
bonita, you, *la bonita* carrying
the clothes. Did you know
I've always admired water,
how it can never be
crushed; it always finds a way
in and out. Nothing is impossible
if you look at the world that way.
I might be ink. I can be the shirt
you sleep in. Even erase you from the street,
this desert city with its Haboob

moving the border across the horizon
and turning red the view, erasing you.
Or I can hold your hand, get lost
tracing your fingers' lengths and follow
your veins' cartography from tip to arm bend,
like a dowser searching
for a trickle, for a subterranean pool
that opens some deep
beyond and forms a stream, a river,
an ocean inside you.
I want to be pulled under.

Portrait of a Dog, Dancing

The sun also clings around the rope's loop, and flies
also twirl and resemble fog this morning.

Sometimes legs lose their desire to dance.
Sometimes no one laughs at a joke.

Ideas spill inside us like a small splash
of wine, the stain a whispered idea

in the neighbor's ear walking home,
and that voice

did not reprimand his clumsy hands
when he unleashed his dog,

and did not speak to the astounded dog
wondering what to do with all the valley before her.

The dog waited and heard no one speaking.
The neighbor waited and listened to the wine's instruction.

Sometimes miracles are not blessings for those
about to die, but for those about to do the killing.

Sometimes we call miracles luck, good or bad. Tonight
call the doorway a miracle where mischief enters,

gives a friendly wink and nudge.
The rope's miracle is its swaying over the rafter

and the neighbor's is that he can stand with so much wine
inside his gut. The rapture comes in the wine's song.

And he hears it. And the dog watches, and both
witness the many miracles of rope.

On the other side of the mountains a ship's wake fans the
    surface of the bay
as it begins a slow hunt for tuna and hake, and the blue

midnight lolls in and out of a porthole glimmering with
    moonlight.
Here the moon wears the rope like a collar, but shrugs it off.

The song tells the man to sit, and he sits.
He watches his lap. Slaps it twice. The dog once

understood this as a word for tenderness, steps closer
as if to better hear, cocks her head as if the slaps were whispers

saying she should expect the man's hand to reach
and stroke that spot behind her ears she dreams sometimes

is touched. It is. The rope, which looked like a porthole
becomes a tender touch and then a collar snugged

around her neck. The dog looks up at the man
looking down. The moon looks down behind him,

and wine laughs inside him at this joke
about a rope and a dog dancing in the moonlight.

The audience of crickets applauds
as the dog reaches her front legs

up, and swallows whistle as rope and wood
filaments and dust flicker down

from above. The man dances with his dog,
holds her paw and leads her through a Paso Doble.

The man shoulders the dog's touch and his chest
accepts the weight of his partner's grasp,

and then her neck, and the dark's touch dizzies him
like a woman reaching her arms out to pull off her dress

and dance with him in the coolness of the valley. The wine's music
turns him to the entry's dark and pirouettes him to a corner of floor.

Sleep. Dreams of dancing and a woman laughing inside
the wine's song are a slow breeze blowing over the dog's ears.

The dog's steps and turns click and score the floor. She glides
and bows, stands straight and turns, forward and back, dips

and twirls through the night until the music stops and the moon sets
behind the mountains and the sun rises, and she tries and she can't.

II.

"I should like to be able to love my country and still love justice."
— Albert Camus

Border Fragments

Moonlight lit dark, inside the coffee cup I carry this morning.
I called it cupped dark the moment I saw it but that moment
    passed.

I once called a night in another country African, but now
I wonder if that sounds racist or if it is international news?

I read the papers in two languages, translate, which is a type of
    border between
truth and fiction, front page news and obituaries, or dispatches
    from each war.

I'll translate this for you: surface and depth.
That's not right. Maybe

mineral and the mine
or the company executive and the Peruvian miner eating his shirt,

or the tourist buying the miner dynamite and *agua
ardiente*. Water burning.

Africa is a crowd of men teetering on a fence south of a place
        I've lived, or
a rush at a border crossing at dawn.

Behind some borders
you can hear the earth moving.

To save yourself from a stampede—Westerns teach us this—climb
a tree, or a rock face, i.e. get out of the way.

The border police watch Westerns in the customs shack
but there are no cattle running below them,

though some women carry children inside them, some men have
sired many children. Other men at times still describe humans
    as stock.

Fences do not stop a stampede. Something magical does—
fatigue, which is an ecstasy of running, of fear.

Or rounds not fired in the air but at the horizon.
Or a rubber bullet hitting high on the cheekbone.

Why is the horizon moving? one border officer asks another.
It sounds like a joke and the other doesn't hear the punch line.

A fence becomes a place to wait, climb,
to guard, to defend. Or turn away from.

The passport stamp inkpad is dry, the walls echo
no stamp slaps on paper. So much moon

light the night could be day. The men so dark they could be
        wearing night.
Blood moon. An eclipse. Everyone looks up.

The men have names. They will be fathers and brothers. Sons
one day will hold their hands and husbands and friends,
        praying at their graves, will remember some night
        they looked up as the mood went dark—the moon,
        I meant to say the moon—as they ran together and
        climbed a fence and sat on the sharp-tipped top as
        light slivered back across their faces, across the sky,
        across a shore like harsh waves send up salt spray.

Peaks of white. Harsh in the night, pain in open wounds that
    one day scar.
A scar is a border.

The street, a fence, an office door threshold and table edge.
A rule, like *You have until 5:00 p.m. to submit your
    paperwork* is also a limit, a border, a place among
    beginnings and ends.

The body. Illegal. My hand there about to, but not touching,
    a boundary between bicep and
    forearm, shoulder and neck.
An embrace, a border closing.

Attrition

A dark morning
seeps, pulls
from inside
of night earth's
black dirt,
the ground
slide budging
slow to erosion.
Call it rolling
over, call it
attrition, call it
loam breath.
Ground thought
or a yard well
no one bothered
to fill and someone
will carry blame
for the dark
that seeped out
and tripped
the man walking by.

American Selfie

Who is the man, for it can only be a man
my head thinks, that would touch a child,

that would strip that child, that would
bend that child over and

would bend that child over
and pierce her and him and him

and her and would turn to this
and that child's mother, who

held by straps and a chair, would become
as lifeless as chairs, as empty as chairs

other mothers refuse to sit in,
but will, and will be forced to watch

quietly like we do at the movies or in a museum,
what is the man that would seem to smile

for those mothers while piercing this and that child,
but does not and does not at the children who must

now be silently heaving having wept dry the tear pools
inside them, but for the camera in the hands of another

man behind those mothers, taking pictures, snap-
shots, souvenirs to take home to their friends,

family and keep in a shoebox that one day,
when that man is old, has forgotten what he has done,

because this breed of man can forget what he has
done, will hold his children's children, who one day

find that curiously stuffed box in a closet, if closets
and shoeboxes and photographs will exist then,

and pull it down in their boredom, open it and see
what their grandfather, what his friends and their

granddaddy did in their boredom
in the name of their country.

Justice—Variations

The boy is twelve and he forgot he was once
six. He was four before that.

The boy shifts the ball he liked to kick and watches his shoes
like a tired paper picker waiting for a meal,

looks down, is quiet as a broken doll
forgotten in light rain.

Night has an age but no one knows it.
The boy doesn't,

though he knows night comes from light's absence,
that quiet sometimes enters a room slowly, locks the door

behind it, waits.
It has approached even when the boy wasn't sleeping. The boy

knows time passes quickly when he sleeps, knows how
sleep can be a blanket if he wants.

Blankets have many uses, and so did the boy have
a father, his father had a friend, that friend was friends with a judge.

Justice in all variations is glint and shadow
and poverty. A boy

is sometimes more than what his body says. In a school yard
knowing a judge does not keep a jury of fists

from writing their verdict on your face,
but a courtroom is not a schoolyard

and a judge is not a friend
most of the time,

does not lose his breath or bloody his knuckles
on his bench. Which is harder to imagine,

six years in the future when a boy is six, or
six years in the past when a boy is twelve?

Or is a boy, once his body's damaged by his father,
damaged less by his father's friend?

Harm sees its face
in punishment's mirror. Waiting

for the lock click to uncover the quiet
inside the room's dark and for that quiet

to be covered again
is longer than a sentence the judge gives his friend.

Justice can be a sentence. A sentence
should hold a subject and predicate.

"The judge reduced the sentence,"
is simple.

"Mario T.,

     director of a football club condemned
     for molesting a boy,

received a reduced sentence

    from the judge, who said the crime is not *gravely*
    offensive because the boy had been
    raped by his father first, and he had *inclinations*, and
    he liked to dress in dresses,"

is a complex sentence.

An unfamiliar room fills. It is an immense room
and in one chair a boy sits. He thinks someone thinks

he has done something wrong. He knows how to say yes.
He knows his age. He looks at his hands.

Border Selfie

"The images of 187 immigrants racing through the Tarajal pass on Monday, which showed two agents kicking and hitting the foreigners with cudgets/truncheons/ clubs generated initial responses yesterday. The Left demanded the Interior Minister clarify/dilute/water down/rinse/ shed light upon the "episode/ occurrence/blip/ incident," and the Unity Party accused the Executive/ Executive Order/ Executive Branch/ Government of lying to hide /disguise/dissemble/ efface/ obscure/paper over/cloak/place out of site/bottle up/conceal the police procedure/ operation/intervention/ involvement. Several ONGs reported/blew the whistle/ informed/ decried/ tattled/ reported that there was an unwarranted/unfair/ uncalled for/unmitigated/ wrongful/unjustified use of force." *El País* 08-09-17

The cameras here

| caught |
| captured |
| understood |

how a policeman

hits	*
bashes	
bonks	
buffets	
smites	
thwacks	

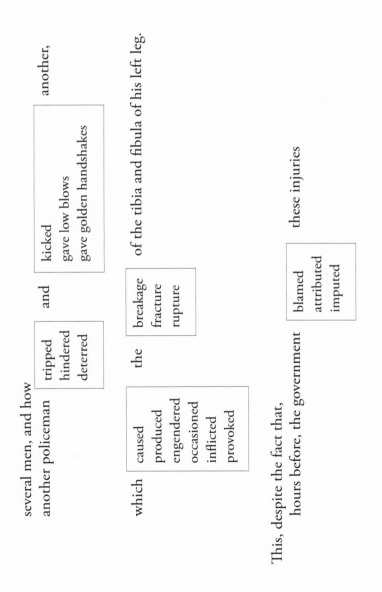

several men, and how

another policeman | tripped / hindered / deterred | and | kicked / gave low blows / gave golden handshakes | another,

which | caused / produced / engendered / occasioned / inflicted / provoked | the | breakage / fracture / rupture | of the tibia and fibula of his left leg.

This, despite the fact that,
hours before, the government | blamed / attributed / imputed | these injuries

49

on/to the "violent

attitude—bad, laid-back, mental, negative, relaxed
outlook
animus
mindset
posture
carriage
artificial horizon
theatrical manner
stance
cautious approach
change of heart
condescending manner
low profile
openness

"

of the foreigners

who

| mowed down |
| swept along |
| dug underneath |
| crushed |
| destroyed |
| brushed aside |
| dominated |

the officers.

Last Monday a group
of close to 200 illegals

| hurried—away from /through/ into |
| foot raced—over |
| rushed |
| scuttled—across |
| hurdled—over |
| dashed—away from/through/into |

the border crossing

51

after security forces had

| deployed |
| extended |
| spread |
| stretched |
| unfolded |
| unfurled |
| opened out |
| dropped down |
| taken wing |

to another part of the fence
where the only blind

| spot |
| corner |
| wall |
| side |
| cesspool |
| double-blind |

in the perimeter is

| found |
| located |
| bumped into |
| blundered into |
| come—across/face-to-face with/ in contact with |
| discovered |
| encountered |
| happened—on/upon |
| met—with/up with |
| run—into/against |

.

One side says "It's unacceptable to try to stop the entrance of migrants, immigrants and possible refugees

| based on |
| on the basis of |
| through |
| by |

(see *)."

.

The other side defends, for their part, the actions of the officers,

| classifying |
| labeling |
| marking |
| rating |
| scoring |

them as

| fitting |
| good |
| polite |
| correct |
| proper |
| regular |
| right |
| right minded |
| well formed |
| right and proper |
| right on |
| wide of the mark |
| politically correct |

A Poem for One of the Men Who Raised Me

If this man wrote a poem it would open a gallon of whole milk and
sprinkle in a thick pinch of salt and not care who else wants a drink.

If this man wrote a poem it would shout ████, ████, ████, &
████ ‡ while he sleeps, in the quiet of his home in front of the TV,
& laugh.

This man's poem would grow soft around the gut—two hundred
seventy-five pounds of soft—but stay lean-and-muscular-cocky
like an angry teen who would pick a fight with any of you ████ §
& pound your ████ ** with his little finger, maybe his Zippo.

A poem by one of the men who raised me would be feared for half
its rotting life until some misstep, some clod in the mouth,
some shove & push & tossed off ████ †† is given back & back
harder & he falls, crumbles & sprawls alone on the ground
surprised by the gravel bits on his collar & indenting his palms.

If some day you are walking in spring & you hear a whimper, look
down because this man, one of the men who raised me, his poem
will lay at your feet, its edges & corners bent, smoldering, brown
& the words in this man's poem will be soft, as if whispered, as if
uncertain, as if regretting some, or maybe all its past speech, & it
should be searching for that deep hole where we buried the rest of him.

---

‡ Read *every kind of racist and homophobic and sexist insult* here
§ ibid
** ibid
†† ibid

To Whoever Stole My Bike Seat

I am sorry, but I do not want to be friends,
or know momentarily your situation
because I am not kind when enraged,
if you give me a chance and come back
for my tire, or the basket for my books
I will greet you with the machete I keep
sharp even in winter when the cactus
is not growing into my neighbor's yard
and I will bury it into your thigh, or swing
up low and crack you a little more, split you
in chunks from the bottom up (yes,
it is that sharp), but do not worry, I will
not kill you, though it kills me a little
to say this, because I do not want to meet
your family who will come to gather your
bleeding parts because I do not want to see
they are starving small starvations you think
a stolen bike seat would have paid for
another meal, or that little Jimmy's Huffy
came without a seat and your wisdom led you
to believe mine would fit his little ass,
which reminds me, asshole, where did you
wait when I left the house, from where
did you watch in this deserted neighborhood
with so little space for hiding, was it
in your truck or were you on your own bike
biking by and saw my back to you walking
north and the woman in the front blue
room working so comfortably under her blue
blanket in a chair you knew she would not rise
to check on a locked bike under the carport,
under the jagged icicles diminishing

onto the seat now in your hands, in which I hope,
at this hour your head is held as your eyes
gaze at the seat that still isn't yours, but mine,
on your coffee table, the seat that has carried
my weight, absorbed parts of me in this heat
and cold any rubbing won't remove, do not
remove your hands from that head of yours
because you will need all of what little you have
there to remember not to ride by here again,
not today or tomorrow or even in the spring
when the heat comes back because this stark,
this stupor you gave me this afternoon
in exchange requires that I stand today like
a snow-stormed man in the driveway in this
sudden West Texas blizzard, tomorrow a little
colder and in the deep rippling heat of July,
colder still, watching for you to coast by
watching me—I will know it is you and you
will know I can ride a bike with no seat, and
I will catch you. I will take back what is
not necessary, what I once possessed.

Coffee in the Dark

Sometimes
          nothing's what I try to hear,
this room smoked, paling, empty before dawn.

                   One
quick flame dimmed to ember glow ate
the cigarette. Four more in twenty minutes
         I got to, he exhales,

empty something big
         before angrying on your face
for what you do. Or don't. The ashtray

              he points to
full of mashed-down paper and ash.
         I've weakened men

with these fists. Want some of this
         ironed cross your jaw, boy?
Again? Don't spit no, "didn't knows" to save your skin

a heavy bruise. Smoke licks up the kitchen
dark. An ember crushed still glows.
              Chair

your ass till I let you stand. Mine,
         hear me?
I know why your lip sweats, what blames you

fear. This hand's gonna place some fear on your eye
you look at me like that. Them hogs hungryed
         a week and I'm trucking

to feed you and you ain't even mine. Your face's
gonna hold a whole glow of swell

today. You better

swallow what you want to say or I'm gonna hard
on you like you've never felt any July sun

on your back,

or a red wing black peck your eye.
Want to
is what I mean. I won't this time, but I want to.

Río Manzanares

Houses here have roofs so frail you pray no moonlight falls
          on them.
They came upon the child sprawled beside the river. A few
cricket clicks this afternoon and sweet whiffs of cattle. You would
wager your hands against how men become monsters. You
          defeat rage
by hiking to the clearing—it happened there and you lay there—
embracing the hollow the body in the coffin made.

People hurt each other everywhere. Unless it's on TV you
          don't know
how hurt feels. They win awards, and respect from the critics. Here,
see them in idling cars on empty roads, night snapping down hard
like a box trap around them. Mothers shriek for fourteen days
          and never speak
the name the same again. Here, that child will never grow older.

To walk along a river bend you acquire it—the switchgrass
          and thicket
and the chain linked fence behind it, humid air that sweats through
your shirt when July shade is impossible. July is one of your
          possessions
now. You possess the repair of every roof you've patched. To get
          by, hold
your own hand. Watch the river currents. Catfish, shallow pool,
          reeds: watch them.

Mujer Cisne

Stop looking away, her plinking change song sings.

You passed her several blocks back.
This swan woman standing
along Constitución rattling her cup of coins.

Imagine her elegance, plink plink
displacing dawn pond water, plink plink
her water-stippled feathers refracting light.

Or was she walking a so slow walk
that looked like standing? Her hair—
a plume black-wrapped in strands
of discarded scarf—leaked down
in tan to sleek her neck and broaden
her shoulder's breadth, her white
shirt stain-faded, and blue dress
stained confused ochre. No
a dress would cover her blonde
legs and keep coins from her cup.
She wears a ripped cloth cinched tight.

Look at my legs, plink plink
exposed for you,
your pity and coins, plink plink
I want plink plink *your disgust.*

I don't sing, her cup sings in cisne tongue,
for who bent it back when I was young
and bones would bend but would not break.
He gave this gift to me—a waddle
like a swan padding on sharp rocks

walks out of water.
I sing for the other who touches my neck
Only for him I give nothing back.

plink plink *I'm unfit for sight out here*
plink *Throw me some place wet*
plink plink *And bless me*
plink *Watch me swim*
plink *Away*

Exile

I walk to the park
edge again, wait
for the Dodge
Street traffic, again
stop and listen to ice
slips and to the black
locust and elm branches
the crows watched
earlier. The sun sets
again over the mall
and a full moon rises
above Summit Street
like no other night I have
seen. Snow sucks my feet,
the wind takes back one
step for every two I take.

The Kind of Man I Used to Be

At that other point in my life, I admit,
I would have killed without second

thoughts, seeing an orange moth clinging
to the yellow dishcloth drying
on the balcony, called it a bug,

pressed my thumb down hard against it
and moved through my day inconsiderate,
killing what else crossed my path.

That is the kind of man I used to be.
I've stepped over it twice, carrying
line-dried shirts and underwear inside.

Do moths divide race by color— this one
dead and that one living beside the door?
I should know why I do what I do, have done.

Did I want to nudge it away, that curiosity
filling this hundredth of an ounce of life,
and thoughts, as I extended

my stupid white finger, about death
as I reached and it reached for me,
touched what once pulled triggers

with its sliver of leg so small I felt nothing
and was surprised such a thing could move,
slap and move back, a gesture that makes me

think if this dust speckle light-as-an-eyelash-flutter
had been wearing pants it would have
put its hand in its pockets, shifted on its legs

and looked cockeyed at me
before skittering away like it did. What could I
do but praise you, all the dead I know,

suddenly alive in the little sifting of wing
and cusp this morning, so I breathe down
on your wings, little shrapnel, half milligrams

of nothing that could harm me, a breath
that translates into some movement
that looks like life in you, flitters your wings

as if some miniscule pulse inside tried to beat
its way out, push against this page you rest upon,
over the words "water, over another country"

and away from the glass door you hit hard
enough to flatten your life out in a second's fractal
of force, delete your breath, subtract the little

that lived inside you from itself, until the nothing
that remains in my palm is heavier than the air
I blow you into, that twirls you to the soft grass below.

Falling for the Woman Walking by the Deadwood

There's a woman out there
who makes me think of Neil
Diamond's glitter and sideburns,
his so white, so un-hip shimmy
to *They're Coming to America*
on American Bandstand. Her
face, she's smiling, talking
to herself, and she isn't the one
I'm waiting for—that one left
my house as I was leaving, ours
an every day cleaving.
                      I like the word
catalyst, that one element creates
a spark, makes something unusual,
something impossible possible, like
an afternoon affair, walking out
one door and through another, a palm
on a stomach as the light shirt above
massages the knuckles, a new wrist,
and how that foreign skin's touch
changes the street grit and noise to luster
and song, how breath enters my lungs
deeply and boils up details I've forgotten,

like the juice lingering from rubbing lilac
blooms between my fingers, how
the hitch in my shadow's step makes
my heart stop for a moment, and how I
can't explain the nerves exploding
in my hands that make desire touch.

No invitation's on her lips,
just a melody I can't hear.
I can't get it out of my head, either.

She's humming. I'm certain of this,
her breath, that air lilting on her lips
breathed to move my eyes off the page,
out this window to her, this woman
I've been waiting for.

This is Midwest love tonight in a bar.
Call it watching and waiting
becomes the consequence.

Happy, TX

Wrench clank, cotton dust, truck exhaust: these
are debts I've paid. The grass here so fragile
I need white gloves to touch it, and I touch

to believe. Geese fly beyond this south and the cold
settled around the lakeshores once they left. I'd stand
like a horizon to own a little space but I salvage

what I've lost by going back, root my feet in the earth,
hold fast to one place. Become part of the terrain. People
walk in woods, around tracks, and through pastures.

Only the poor like me stand still, even in our moving
there is slow standing— each step a slab of earth.
We own where we stand, where we squat. Here in

Happy I am iron until someone stops or looks long,
then I float and dissipate into red dirt dust. No one
mourns my leaving. I walk like dead weeds scatter.

Tumble away. But tumble slowly along ridge and
hollow and machine shop grit, rusty barrel dents,
the visiting whore's boa's shadow lifting and falling

in the wind, and scratching tires and pebble spatter
of passing traffic heading away to own some other
space. Where I stand is home. I own part of what I see.

Selfie in Dark Interior

Before, ache never seemed long like a tunnel
under the city flaring off another tunnel
the subway rumbled against, or the dark

jutting out of daylight's reach up on 187th
when I know some part is inhabited and
that habitation looks out at me. I know

every uninhabited place lodges a thing looking
out. I have grown into a life, become middle
aged, deepened into the hidden inside, like

the day into its other half, or a memory
of a woman's silence after she didn't
want to be kissed, and I wonder when rot

began, and I wonder what other ideas the cabbie
had when he turned into the truck's path.
Sometimes silence is emptier than some oaths

I have made. Hours change habits and late seeps
into early and rain, in another part of this
country, suddenly, heavily falls, flattens seams,

frays and splits them the way I did away from a lover
once in a city where both of us were foreign, and she
the only person who recognized me for a thousand miles,

the only one who knew where I was. And
then not. This ache is empty like that.

III.

"My past is everything I failed to be."
— Fernando Pessoa

Selfie with Goathead

—for my daughter

The plague lies under sumac, under foxtail, under Mule-
shoe's other weeds she tamps down in her forth

and back sauntering. Mornings she shouts at the dark
then looks out of the dark at me, deskbound and comes,

climbs the chair and cat-like kneads my lap, curls and pushes
her stretch into me. It's not why I look up foxtail, but

why I read about grasses we call weeds and dogs and danger
            and believe
she too could die from what creeps forward

never back, might be the cause of her sneeze
                                        sometimes in my face.

I pick her up, place her behind me, lean
forward in my chair so she can feel my back.

She likes touch, could call it *cozy* in a language she'll learn to
            speak. Every good
feeling carries excessive weight, carries some dust of suffer. This

thing I love could be my bag, a living thing mine. I own
her. Men used to own other men. My stepfather told me that

one time—*I own you, boy,* thumbing iambs on my skull;
you're mine until you leave this house. I own you, your

time, all you will do. Mine. Variation, a gesture to shift, and men
own wives still. Not over there where language sounds like anger,

but here I've heard "she's my woman," and I own

　　　　　　　　　　　　　　　　plenty. This pen.

This cup, the snot in a wad of tissue the dog tries to eat from my pocket.
So much paper a forest presses the shelves and table top down

more than gravity. That doesn't make sense—gravity. To be weighed
down. The implication of falling back, to earth, to something heavier

than what is not. My dog to me, my arms to the back of my chair
she wants to occupy though her pad is empty at my feet.

It's about touch. Touch at 4:00 a.m. when the night seems long
and she's alone. I'm alone too but forget that, forget that

one thing so filled with another the outside seems occupied,
infested as she was with goatheads so I picked her up,

carried her and plucked them from her coat. They drew my blood.
They carried it falling to the ground. My blood,

a pollen for the dangerous seeds I dropped. A sprig
of pain will grow from there. A vast national park of pain

is growing in this country where I live. No one I know tends
or nurtures it, pain I mean, but someone does. Someone always does.

First Dust Storm

Is it a Nuthatch? Is it a Grackle—
female—I can't tell which bird
is which though they look
at each other and see no other
friend or self as if in a mirror,
like Patricio says to me, *You*
white boys all look alike
and that used to bother me
most of all because
in Williamsburg all of us
did look like brothers
and all of us in Pella and all of us
in Donostia, too, though they
were not white like the white he saw
as Basques and their noses looked
more like Patricio's, but that's not true
either; his looks like an F turned
upside down and smashed flat,
like a standard Cooper Black, so black
and pressed I do double takes when I look
at my font book and print out Fs
when I miss him and turn them
upside down on chairs, and I'll talk
to them and wish he were here
and suddenly there's dirt outside
the window moving fast, about
to boil over the pot the day is
on this West Texas stove. Run,
I say to the birds on the porch.
Fly away is what I mean
and they understand, fly away
and get tossed like little air bubbles

toiling to the surface in a fish tank,
which this place has become,
but I don't know if I'm outside
looking in at the murk and all
the trouble's frothing and splashing
about, or if that's the way
the world looks to those who are
held inside, like I am in this house
beside the clear windows moving
back and forth from view to view.

On Finding Myself in Wrong Places

Like at a back-corner library
carrel beside a sneezing woman
drinking can after can of V8
and the tobacco chewing
and spitting straw-colored
man with green ear buds
and then the librarians, each
propping the door open
with those little rubber triangles
I once told a woman my father
invented and that's why
we're millionaires,
and why prop an office door open
if you're going to talk? I feel
no remorse when I stand finally
and go to one office and ask
if the woman whispering
loudly will shut her door
while the other sits behind her
desk. One had a cane
and the other contempt
in her eyes, or just eyes
set off by a terrible haircut
and I almost bend down
to unplug that triangle
from the door but I saw
myself doing it and why
would I kneel before these
two women who are not quiet
librarians, and on the other side
the woman has finished her V8s
and two men, two more librarians

had entered another office
and propped open the door
and one of them, the older,
wider one, asked the thin
rail of a man *who do you think*
voted against me? What
does that mean? And the other
mumbled something so thin
I couldn't hear it, thin like his wife
who when they walk by my house
I think of two exclamation marks,
and he has cat posters hanging
on his walls and the other
looks angry, as if he hated
those cat posters, too,
and then a large woman comes
along after the thin man leaves
and shuts the door, stubbing
the little triangle with one easy kick
and the door does fill the doorway
suddenly but it has no insulation
against her words and works like
a magnifying glass and I've never
heard a young woman speak
to an old man that way
so I was momentarily
uncomfortable and the man
with the green ear buds left
and another woman looked
over the top of the carrel wall
at me as if I had something to do
with it, and the volume grew

and the big woman sounded
like she was speaking out of her body
and the old man was quieting,
but still grasping at something,
as if a corner of his desk,
as if he might be about to fall
from some great height, a mountain
in there, urgent were his words
and distant like they were also falling
and finally she opened the door
and slammed it and the mountain trembled
from that slam, from that voice
that might have echoed God's
if you believe what Moses said, and
the man and all the other voices were
suppressed like a flame snuffed out,
and the library went back to quiet,
the way that bush Moses saw
became just another mountain bush.

Ode to Not Writing the Perfect Poem

Instead of putting down my friend's book midway through
a poem that itches me around in my seat,
I honor him, his worlds and song and read on through each line

and slap my knee joyful he's so fucking smart and speaks beautiful
words I want to sing praises and play a harp or shoot some heroin
and linger a bit so when I read him again, especially now that I have

forgotten another perfect line he almost helped my finger scribble,
the one that would make the world inside spin gravity out, hold
miracles down like basil perfume on a sweaty woman's wrist

she rubs across her cheek to wipe that glistening away
in a September yard or somewhere north, because this
world has cardinal directions, too, a mound of flower buds

from a jasmine-like bush in delicious scented
circles painting white the soil a dog rolls around so giddy in
that stink, pleased with himself he has found it before anyone else,

and has ownership over it, and he carries that funk with him
through the day smiling and laughing so hard his tongue touches
the street when he walks, you would too if you could

lick your own balls, if you could wear a coat all the time and pee
and shit where you want and get stuck inside your lover
and have to wait the certain time it takes for love to unswell

your panting, settle that muscle you have no more control over
than that poem your friend has written, that you can't put down
and you sacrifice your own possible excellence to praise his,

to feel it shimmer inside your lungs and catch your breath,
take hold of you and then leave you breathless,
and then leave you standing and panting right where you are.

Fuck Spring

No, I mean it.
I wish
I could pull
his pants
off, throw him on
his back
and gloriously,
howlingly fuck
together and let
the day age around us.
Let apricot
blossoms fall
like cotton
chuff in heavy
sunlight
and blanket
our naked plowing.
Let us be root
rough and compact
the dirt. Quake it. Really,
I've never said
this to anyone else,
I'll tell it,
massaging something
like summer heat
into its back, but
I want to fuck you
and get drunk
on that fucking
like bees fondling
the lavender
by the garden hose, or

dip and suck
from the lilac and jasmine
every last staining sweetness.

Sometimes in the Dark

A woman I love says some things
we can't unknow. Sometimes

in the dark, say 2:00 a.m., knowing
too much nudges my shoulder

softly like another woman
I loved never did, bites,

tongues my ear instead, and squirms
sleep out of my chest, and

I try to unsee what's present in the dark
corners—not dust, not some dinner-with-

colleagues receipt but the proficient
force a hand possesses to hit

a cheek and leave no mark,
how stink is a cast around a bone

broken through skin
a man will try to ignore

with a kiss. I have tried
twenty seven times to unfathom

the depth a last breath sounds,
its echo like the sting *I don't love you*

makes resurfacing in my chest.
Unknowing

the faculties of man, those precise lessons
pain handcuffs us to, like a thing once

mishandled wrapped tight in barbwire
corrals us inside a past. I have

mastered simple words. I have learned
to caress tenderness into a wound.

Longing Deconstructed

It was darker then, and we could see lights
speckle in the distance beyond our windows
and bedroom walls. Then gone.
                              When beds
and floors creaked it meant someone was
getting up in the night, leaving, and the low
murmur in the kitchen radio reading markets,
or school cancelations, or hail insurance ads
meant we weren't alone.
                        We never saw anyone
beautiful in our town. Beauty was a foreign word
we couldn't pronounce, like curse words
our parents used in German to hide
the missing rent, unpaid bills, the divorce.
                                            Snow
drifted across the road every year, piled
between the windbreak pine and sifted through
screens to jostle our windows like cats knead
a pillow in the dark.
                      Cats and dogs were not pets,
but animals outside with defining names
like Cat and Dog.
                  One day the clocks stopped
ticking and the rooms lumined dull green
light. Our latitude filled with that glowing.

Family Night Out, Buenos Aires Circa 2015

I would go back if I could sit again
beside a table where a middle-aged
son sat in front of his bent mother,
who sat beside that Brazilian woman
probably hired to care for her
but has now become the middle-
aged son's lover, or wife, and
I'd go back if I could listen
a little more closely to their meal
conversation—*Does this look like*
what I ordered? Ma, how's your omelet?
Could we get some oil and vinegar
for the salad? Does this look
like vinegar? Wait a minute...250 pesos
for this bottle of wine? Are you fu...
I've never had a bottle of 250 peso wine.
Christ!—and I'd stay a little longer,
even order some gin, though I know
better, if I could be settled at a table
with a good angle and watch
the man mumble across the street
to the ramshackle car parked there
while that Brazilian nurse/lover/wife
shuffles in stride with the bent mother
in front of an ambulance—lights flashing
to stop other cars fast approaching—
and across the street to look in the window
of a second-hand furniture store, watch
the woman point at something
with her cane and see instead Stern
gesturing the same indication with his cane
in Lambertville but to a sign

for the Methodist Church, before saying,
Fucking Methodists! for no reason,
or see my mother-in-law on a street
in northern Spain, feel her arm
in the crook of mine as this woman's
is in that Brazilian woman's—two foreigners
with the mothers of the ones they love—
lingering to look at what others have given
up so others might buy, then gripping
a little, which I translate as, *let's move
on a while*, and as I sip that gin
I'd keep watching as they sink
into the car, the car settling and leaning
under their weight, sputtering, rattling,
disappearing down the street, and
instead of getting up to leave I know
I should wait a little longer because gin
needs to settle and events like this never
settle when I think they do, and that car
driven by the muttering son beside his mother,
behind whom sits that Brazilian nurse,
or lover, or wife, who is darker than the two
up front, who because the mother is too old
and because the son is driving, only
because of that, does she get out quickly
and rush to the table minutes before they left,
still cluttered with food they didn't eat,
an empty beer bottle and that 250 peso wine
bottle, still partially full, and grab it and rush back
and slam the door, and she must have shouted
*I've got it, or Drive, for Christ's sake, look out
where yr going,* the way Creeley told someone

and because I've stuck around for this
and the taste of what I have not admitted
is still on my tongue I'll repeat it, too,
I've got it, let's go, and I did and I do.

A Sound Like a River

There's a stretch called nothing
between Carlsbad and El Paso
and I'm thinking while my wife
is in the back seat with Ibai
that the SUV we passed forty
or fifty miles back driving
and stopping through town
might have taken some offense
with my gaze and smirk and in
the miserable night this has become
in southern New Mexico lit only
by its headlights in my rearview
mirror where I see the dog in
my wife's arms ready to vomit
on her and the leather seats and
we are close to the border and close
to being farthest from everything
known and no one knowing where
we are, aren't we every day on some
edge of disappearing somehow
and maybe Ibai feels that menace, too,
and vanishing is her first memory
or maybe she only has to pee and wants
the dark curves to flatten out.
                              Sometimes
when she sleeps she looks like she is
running and then she's swimming or
flailing that first swim of hers out
of the valley stream she was thrown in
with her brothers and sisters because
rushing water washes away what some
men want to disappear and her litter

mates disappeared under a dark sound
and we call her what the Basque call
river because Erreka was too harsh
for the puppy she was then and who
could shout it anyway in that moment
she must stop chasing a moth, drop
some blue bumblebee pacifier
she's found in the street, or if
she's shitting on the bed. Tonight the wind
rushes through the open window like stream
water does down mountains, a resonance
in the dark she wants to run from but can't.

Stupid Job

I'm a liar. It's not a job
that pays well but I am
my own boss. My wife
brushes teeth. Hers. She
flosses, too. I've asked her
to do mine. *Get a job*,
she tells me. *I have one.*
I'm a liar, I tell her. We
look at each other, as if
we were paintings, as if
looking would make clear
some deep meaning,
make us smarter,
make us at least feel
better about ourselves.

If Brueghel Had Painted an Iowa Landscape

He would now focus on the streetlights in the dark,
all of them red, everyone held inside their waiting. No
thing mimicking the stars' glimmer and the crows gathered
in the trees around the library in the middle of town
preening, watching, preening. A caw about to crack
the night open, and a bell toll, and a compact thunk
about to drop behind a shed. A convenience store
owner gives a little solitude away with each Big Gulp
and gallon of gas. Smells are free but hard to paint.
Dogs sniff each other's necks and backs and butts
on a north corner of Avenue B and C Street,
the concrete virgin raises her hand to bless them,
the sidewalk, the otherwise empty street except
for a man walking home with a six-pack and
a Barbie doll he picked up in the alley behind the Broken
Spoke. Brueghel would have painted the town edged
by wide corn and hay and soybean fields and the man's lips
moist from sipping *Old Milwaukee*. He would have
painted barn swallows circling a hay field, cowbirds
chattering in cottonwood and box elder branches watching
this man speak little words to the doll, *My daughter*
will comb and brush your pretty hair and dress you
for dates and balls. One fence marks a frontier
between two feuding farmers' ground, two fences
confine the family histories inside them. He would have
painted heat boiling inside this man by unbuttoning
his shirt, rolling in little folds his sleeves, and the widow
of the man he worked for on a porch swing, feet raised,
shoeless, pale under a glowing yard light. At one corner
a tractor's lights outline dust rising on a field lane. Here
the painter would have stopped to consider light and dark
and the story buried inside oil or tempera paint he layers,

brushes and scrapes to expose. Just as debt conceives
consequence a day empties completely at some hour,
therefore crows remain black specks in black trees,
beside black fields under a blanket of stars, which are
absences inside the dark, like a man on a horizon at the far end
of an alley, grown so small he becomes a dull glint on the can
raised to his mouth, like light before dawn, or long after dusk.

Three Sketches of Anxiety

I've got two hands and an urge
to yank out your teeth,

my lover said, dropping the dress
she made from my shirt

to the floor, *to see the landscape*
a mouth of holes might look like.

Maybe jagged potholes on a rain-
slick street, she said, climbing over

the bed. *Maybe*, she winked, *a prairie*
dog town in West Texas after a flood.

Lines Regarding the Black Feathers on Canton

Soon enough the grackles will truth
the yard out back beneath the wires,

the sidewalk cracks, the live oak roots.
They will lose their dying feathers, now glossed

the greasy sheen the females polish
their beaks with. They must be blind,

or like a shiny bone. Or they mistake
the burr and clatter from the other's

throat for song, the clamor a talisman
that pulls them in. Like a lover might

feel the pulse in the other's arm
and want to hold it tighter, let

the beating become a surging matched
in her chest. When I pass the grackles

on 21st, they turn and watch me pass
like the crows back in Oskaloosa

used to, looking down on me, the only man
walking those bleak streets, watch.

Silence here can needle into the cracks
and weaken a structure's core. Like water

erodes every solid, can wear it paper thin.
A song a woman sang me once, a tender

orchid of a song so delicate I thought hearing
it would wilt every molecule of its beauty, did this,

too. The voice that bloomed the song's flower
today became the grackle explosion and call.

Career Change

I tried to write a letter. I can't.
I'm thirsty instead. I walked

around all day. My wife's
gone again and I'm a liar.

But no news there—I need
to hold a woman's hand

again, squeeze her fingers,
feel some warmth before

the weather changes.
I'd hug her, too and watch

the trees blow in and out
of the window frame

behind her instead of closing
my eyes. I'm in trouble,

I say.
            When I had a job

I didn't think about such things,
then one day I started thinking.

Everything went to hell
after that. I acquired tastes

and heard voices that got me
drunk and suggested that

maybe I should stop working.
So I stopped working—I read

the warning signs on the forklift:
Do not operate under the influence,

so I stopped operating. The boxes
got too heavy.
                              Now I teach.
No one knows the difference.

Three Abstractions of Light

The horizon, a slow darkness hovering before and behind space hinged inside a view unlit by streets.

There is no light before or after sunrise so violet as if light could be an extract of vanilla or almond—essence of woman's breast, concentrate of crotch, distillate of pubis, nape tincture.

Ideas reoccur in my hands, evidence of each word's obligation.

I press close to this fear of sight leaving my eyes, like a moth must want closer to anxiety light ticks its soft skull against as if to push it away.

Violet on the desert, ground hugging, a flower's dark moving to light's inverse inside its petals, like a woman I never kissed who made a cake ornamented with violets.

For me. *Eat. Eat them*, she said.
And I did.

I was always thirsty then, and today, how many days after
the first day of fall, there are no more violets anywhere.

The sun, the horizon a kind of nod like a blind man on a street, turning
his head side to side as if thinking No.

No.
No could look like that.

There is a name for that, a condition I don't know what to call,
just as a better definition of this time will occur,

or how light falls through a glass pane and refracts
into a building under construction, the street below

crossed by utility lines, shreds the wall with shadow.
This piece touched, this untouched.

101

A blind man in Iowa City all one summer asked people passing through College Street Park about the tall man with the deep voice.

If I can believe in the existence of a color, I can believe the blind can see as easily as the seeing do.

That blind man asked to see my face. Unfamiliar with such a request, to look, I nodded, said yes.

His fingers saw my cheeks first, then my chin, traced my jaw to my ears, looked across my temples, under my eyes,

up the bridge my nose makes across my brow, then that beach of skin before the sea of hair I have.

He called my hair a sea, and ran his hands through it like lovers have.

Both hands meeting
at the back of my neck.

We stood, my eyes closed, his open,
both in the dark of some other place.

ʅ

In this new country I don't know
if I look East or West from here.

A man should know
how to look.

Direction is a possession,
acquired and carried.

And can't the blind know, too?

Walking east and feeling the rising sun's heat kiss that beach of forehead, the heat of something
like hands falling away from your neck, from the earth beneath us leading somewhere.

Coffee stain on my finger.
Writing on my hand.

103

A tattoo of to dos I haven't done. I can't hear light, or taste it
in the coffee my lover says she tastes on my lips.

There is morning there, she says, licking her own after we kiss.
It hasn't been dark for hours by that time.

I've already thought of two other women.
There will be others today.

And men. And the dog I watched fall from the sky
on television, so calm I imagine he might talk to me

and I wouldn't be surprised.
And bombs falling on children don't surprise me.

Or men knowing they can rape women and walk back into their lives, buy cars,
deodorant, life insurance plans and parent happy children, none of it surprises me.

A sudden blue jay scream in the silence
and I hadn't realized the dark leaving the yard

reminded me the man I saw four days ago
at the end of the neighbor's drive,

arms at his side, was shaking his head
at the horizon the sun would settle

then erase. I watched him in the car mirror
look at me driving to that light. He couldn't shake it loose.

Another Woman I Loved

This was bitter—the rain pouring down on us,
the too early risers, waiting in line outside
the National Portrait Gallery. Flood-
like; movie-like (Why would you want to live there?
my brother asked. It's always raining); and
just like the movies, I had an umbrella
and she didn't, she had looks, and I didn't,
wanted to practice her already perfect English,
understood her body exactly, and I didn't.
I gestured, held the umbrella out to her
and she took my arm, we waited together,
not talking about the weather or both being
foreign, but the familiar smells we missed
from home and when we last caught them
here, or the bitter tea we couldn't get used to.
Maybe we laughed and I felt even more
of her body next to mine. I have told this story
so many times; some women stay inside a man;
her beauty, of course, was stunning
and I didn't deserve to be near it—her
confidence—though she was sopping wet.
It was her unexpected presence, my arm
was a door she took hold of and opened,
her hand the key; it was
the little dry space and conversation
we shared: she didn't walk away once
inside but waited for me on a bench,
and I didn't rush down a crowded hall, say,
shivering with her perfume still on my shirt,
the memory of her forearm touching my hip,
reeling. I had gone there to look at paintings
and write to another woman.

She had fallen out of love with me and I didn't
see it. I've put this off for years, but now I see
I found a clue, or was given one that morning
and afternoon in central London. I would spend
another day with her, hear her voice on the phone
twice, and then she left. Twenty years ago
I drank my tea and worried across the table
from her, holding my hand; we never met again
although we'd planned to spend a weekend together—
I could have a daughter or son who speak
a language I don't understand, a giggling grandchild,
newborn and soft, smelling like milk and warmth
in Paris or Dubrovnik. Every other year I think
about her, wonder how I could find her, if she is still
singing, still alive, and I tried writing her once.
I did only that. We never shared a room in Ljubljana,
or met in Venice, or swam naked in the Adriatic.
I started thinking of her again this morning.
I still feel that woman's arm between my elbow
and chest. The thought of her grows, sweetens.
There aren't so many women I've loved. I gave
that woman half of me because it wasn't being used.
With that savings, I bought this: the Anjou pear,
a cup of coffee, this red table. I followed her,
eager, joyous. I earned this memory. It must sound
silly. Her beautiful face. Her hand pressed
into mine. Twenty-three rain drops on her hair.

Vermilion Flycatcher

Did I spell that right? One *L* or two? Like
my friend I have doubts about so many things
but also I can't spell in my first, not third
language, and this bird Jim can name
only when he slips back to the Brazil
where he was ten and an uncivilized boy
of missionaries who later sent him north
for its civilization, an education, measures the sounds
of that language I think makes everyone sexy,
makes me anxious and it's already 85 degrees
and March and the cottonwoods are leafing
along the river some illegals follow north,
hide in, and others get this far and go to the park
house canopied by one more giant cottonwood
and say *I quit* in what language they speak for not
every illegal speaks my second language,
but I'll translate anyway into something like
this: *I'll wait here for the migra* [because there
are foreign words in foreign tongues, too] *while you
call and could you bring me some water
and maybe fan my feet?* and these trees
might look like fans and most everyone who needs
to know knows if you see their outline in the distance
you will find water near and if I had ever looked
at the sky through spring cottonwoods before
I'd have said it may be a miracle I shouldn't forget,
but I have never been so thirsty, so illegal or
distracted by magnificence along a river more
like a trickle and wondered how long I'd been
lost and if maybe I'd already crossed the border
and become illegal in a way others are not. Today
I will do something the neighbors back home

would think illegal, but here I'm ignored, looked
over then overlooked, like it's easy to overlook
the vermilion flycatcher's fluttering red blur
amidst so much green, so much dry, *vermelhão*,
an ecstasy, a revolution on the tip of my tongue when I say it.

Notes

"Euphoric" is for Emily

"Returning to a Moment" is written in memory of Jackie Brookner

"Ode to Not Writing the Perfect Poem" is for Salpicón

"What Beauty Is, Is" is for the Basque

"In Praise of Maybe" is for Sebastian

"A Poem for One of the Men Who Raised Me" is after a poem by Gary Jackson

"To Whoever Stole My Bike Seat" is after a poem by Steve Scafidi

"Selfie in Dark Interior" is for Patricio

"On Finding Myself in Wrong Places" is for Gerald Stern

"Three Abstractions of Light" is for Victoria

"Vermilion Flycatcher" is for Jim Graham and Martha Betancourt

Acknowledgments

Thanks to the editors of the publications in which the following poems appeared, though sometimes in a different incarnation and under a different title: *Fulcrum*: "On Forgetting"; *Pinyon*: "Dust Dance"; *The Cortland Review*: "Stupid Job"; *The Common*: "Another Woman I Loved," "Lines Regarding the Black Feathers on Canton" and "Drawing Snow"; *Talking River Review*: "Lines to a Friend in a Less Windy Place"; *The North American Review*: "Rio Manzanares"; *The Oxford American*: "Returning to a Moment"; *Tin House*: "Euphoric" and "Three Sketches of Anxiety"; *The Southern Indiana Review*: "Self Portrait in Dark Interior"; *Tuesday An Art Project*: "The Reason for Your Silence" and "Evensong."

The poems "Stupid Job," "Self Portrait in Dark Interior" and "Lines to a Friend in a Less Windy Place" appear on the Academy of American Poets page. The poem "Selfie with Dust" appears in the chapbook *ground / work*.

I want to give my gratitude to the kind patrons at Residencia Elola-Astiazaran in Atxondo, Euskadi and Residencia Roquissar in Valldemossa, Spain who provided uninterrupted time and beautiful spaces to work on portions of this book; to the Banff International Literary Translation Centre (BILTC) at Banff Centre for Arts and Creativity, Banff, Alberta, Canada, where in addition to translations I also secretly worked on these poems; and to the Vermont Studio Center for the valuable time and space to complete portions of this book, in particular Ryan Walsh, Jody Gladding, and Gary Clark.

I am grateful to more people than I can thank here for their kindness, friendship, and critical wisdom during the writing of this book, though especially I want to thank—my friends and colleagues at *Waxwing* and *The Common*; my colleagues in the Creative Writing and Comparative Literatures programs, the Department of English, the Department of Classical and Modern Languages and Literatures, and the College of Architecture at Texas Tech University; to my graduate and undergraduate students for their exercises and conversations that helped some of these poems come to life; Bruce Clarke and Brian Still for their administrative kindness while I worked to complete this collection; the *Lubbock Scapes Collective* for creating generous and invigorating intellectual and creative space to try out these poems; the Field Office family, and in particular the amazing Vaughan Fielder who brought us together and keeps us in line; thank you Sebastian Matthews, Mira Rosenthal, Rebecca Gayle Howell, Patrick Rosal, Vievee Francis, and Ross Gay, generous poets, translators, readers, and friends who have helped me refine this book, its vision, and space…without your close, bighearted readings of these poems and your encouragement I'm not sure this book would be what it is now; thank you to Jean Valentine, Gerald Stern, Thomas Lux, Robin Becker, Vijay Seshadri, Christopher Merrill, and Barry Lopez for showing me the gift of your kindness and generosity; thank you Peter Covino and Barrow Street Press for being an early and consistent supporter of my work, for believing in this book, for your endless patience with me and my drafts and questions, and for welcoming me into the Barrow Street family.

Finally, thank you Ibai for sticking around, and thank you Idoia, fellow traveler, for allowing me to continue on this journey with you.

Curtis Bauer is the author of *Fence Line* (BkMk Press, 2004) and *The Real Cause for Your Absence* (C&R Press 2013). His translations include: *Eros Is More* (Alice James Books, 2014), by Juan Antonio González Iglesias; *From Behind What Landscape* (Vaso Roto Editions, 2015), by Luis Muñoz; and *Image of Absence* by Jeannnette Clariond (Word Works, 2018). His work has appeared in *Tin House, The Literary Review, Two Lines and The American Poetry Review,* among others. He is Translations Editor for *The Common Magazine* and he teaches Creative Writing and Comparative Literature at Texas Tech University.

Photo by Idoia Elola

BARROW STREET POETRY

American Selfie
Curtis Bauer (2019)

Hold Sway
Sally Ball (2019)

Green Target
Tina Barr (2018)

Adorable Airport
Jacqueline Lyons (2018)

Luminous Debris: New & Selected Legerdemain
Timothy Liu (2018)

We Walk into the Sea: New and Selected Poems
Claudia Keelan (2018)

Whiskey, X-ray, Yankee
Dara-Lyn Shrager (2018)

For the Fire from the Straw
Heidi Lynn Nilsson (2017)

Alma Almanac
Sarah Ann Winn (2017)

A Dangling House
Maeve Kinkead (2017)

Noon until Night
Richard Hoffman (2017)

Kingdom Come Radio Show
Joni Wallace (2016)

In Which I Play the Run Away
Rochelle Hurt (2016)

The Dear Remote Nearness of You
Danielle Legros Georges (2016)

Detainee
Miguel Murphy (2016)

Our Emotions Get Carried Away Beyond Us
Danielle Cadena Deulen (2015)

Radioland
Lesley Wheeler (2015)

Tributary
Kevin McLellan (2015)

Horse Medicine
Doug Anderson (2015)

This Version of Earth
Soraya Shalforoosh (2014)

Unions
Alfred Corn (2014)

O, Heart
Claudia Keelan (2014)

Last Psalm at Sea Level
Meg Day (2014)

Vestigial
Page Hill Starzinger (2013)

You Have to Laugh: New + Selected Poems
Mairéad Byrne (2013)

Wreck Me
Sally Ball (2013)

Blight, Blight, Blight, Ray of Hope
Frank Montesonti (2012)

Self-evident
Scott Hightower (2012)

Emblem
Richard Hoffman (2011)

Mechanical Fireflies
Doug Ramspeck (2011)

Warranty in Zulu
Matthew Gavin Frank (2010)

Heterotopia
Lesley Wheeler (2010)

This Noisy Egg
Nicole Walker (2010)

Black Leapt In
Chris Forhan (2009)

Boy with Flowers
Ely Shipley (2008)